The Solar System

CONTENTS

4-5 The Solar System

6-7 The Sun

8-9 Inside the Sun

10-11 The Outer planets.

12 Jupiter

13 Inside Jupiter

14 Saturn

15 Inside Saturn

16 Uranus

17 Neptune

18-19 The Inner planets

20 Mercury

21 Venus

22-23 Earth

24-25 Inside Earth

26-27 Earth's Moon

28 Mars

29 Inside Mars

30-31 The asteroid belt

THE SOLAR SYSTEM

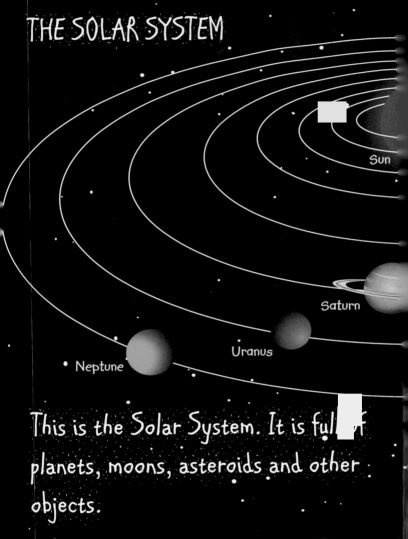

Sun

Saturn

Uranus

• Neptune

This is the Solar System. It is full of planets, moons, asteroids and other objects.

Mercury

Venus

Earth

Mars

Jupiter

Eight planets revolve around the Sun.

5

THE SUN

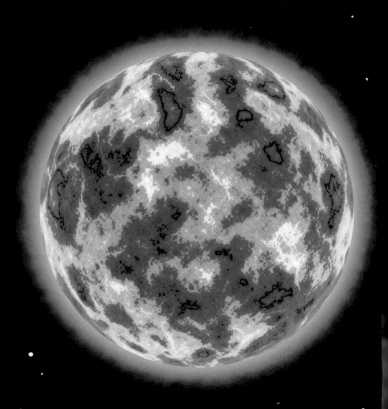

The Sun is a star at the centre of our Solar System. It is a yellow star that gives us heat and light. The Sun is the closest star to Earth. It is more than one hundred times bigger than Earth.

INSIDE THE SUN

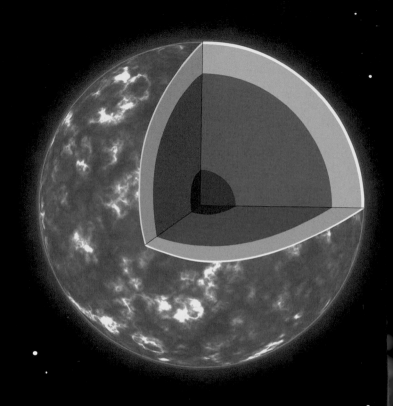

The Sun is like a ball of burning gas. The centre of the Sun is called the core. It is very hot in the core.

THE OUTER PLANETS

Neptune

Uranus

The planets farthest from the Sun are known as the Outer planets.

10

Jupiter

Saturn

Let's look at the
Outer planets.

11

JUPITER

Jupiter is a giant planet. Jupiter has over sixty moons and it spins very quickly.

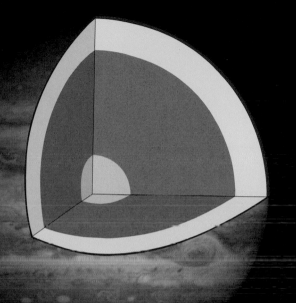

Jupiter is made of gas. It has no surface. It is not possible to land on Jupiter. The core is made of rocky ice.

SATURN

Saturn is the second biggest planet. It has beautiful rings made of chunks of ice and some rocks.

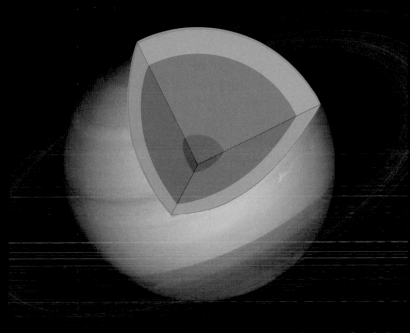

The core of Saturn is rocky. It is very hot at the core.

URANUS

Uranus is made of frozen gas. Its core is made of molten rock and is surrounded by icy water.

Neptune is a giant planet and has eight moons. It is the farthest planet from the Sun.

17

THE INNER PLANETS

Sun

Mercury

The Inner planets are closest to the Sun. Let's look at the Inner planets.

MERCURY

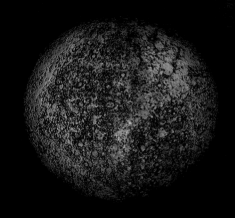

Mercury is the smallest planet in the Solar System. Mercury is the closest planet to the Sun. It has many deep craters. The core is very big and contains a lot of iron.

Venus is a little smaller than Earth.
It has a rocky surface but no craters.
There are many volcanoes on Venus.

EARTH

Earth is the third planet from the Sun. It is the only planet where plants grow and animals live. Earth has huge areas of water and land.

INSIDE EARTH

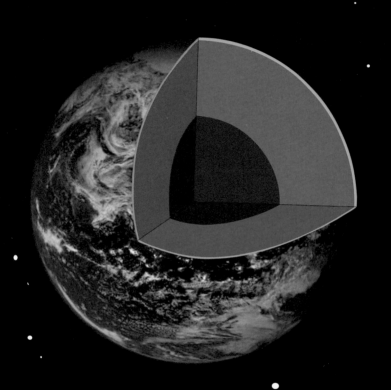

Earth is made up of layers. The core, in the centre, is hotter than the surface of the Sun. The core is surrounded by the mantle and the outer layer is known as the crust.

EARTH'S MOON

Earth has only one moon.
The moon is cold and dry. Its surface
is covered in loose rocks and dust.
The moon has many craters. It takes
one month to travel around Earth.

MARS

Mars is known as the red planet. The surface of Mars is dry and rocky. Mars is a cold planet and has very little air. It has two tiny moons.

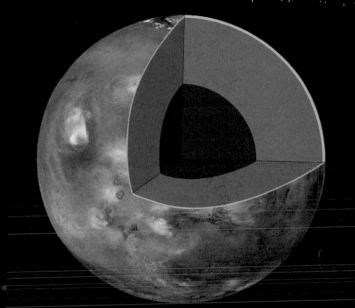

Mars has layers inside just like Earth. These are called the crust, the mantle and the core.

THE ASTEROID BELT

Asteroids are rocky objects.